HISTORY OF FUN STUFF

The Way the Cookie Crumbled

by Jody Jensen Shaffer
illustrated by Kelly Kennedy

Ready-to-Read

Simon Spotlight
New York   London   Toronto   Sydney   New Delhi

SIMON SPOTLIGHT
An imprint of Simon & Schuster Children's Publishing Division
1230 Avenue of the Americas, New York, New York 10020
This Simon Spotlight edition July 2016
Text copyright © 2016 by Simon & Schuster, Inc.
Illustrations copyright © 2016 by Kelly Kennedy
For information about special discounts for bulk purchases, please contact Simon & Schuster Special Sales
at 1-866-506-1949 or business@simonandschuster.com.
The Simon & Schuster Speakers Bureau can bring authors to your live event. For more information or to
book an event, contact the Simon & Schuster Speakers Bureau at 1-866-248-3049 or visit our website at
www.simonspeakers.com.
Manufactured in the United States of America 0516 LAK
2 4 6 8 10 9 7 5 3 1
Library of Congress Cataloging-in-Publication Data
Shaffer, Jody Jensen, author.
The way the cookie crumbled / by Jody Jensen Shaffer ; illustrated by Kelly Kennedy.
pages cm. — (History of fun stuff)
1. Cookies—History. I. Kennedy, Kelly (Illustrator), illustrator. II. Title.
TX772.S4926 2016 641.86'54—dc23 2015033717
ISBN 978-1-4814-6181-8 (hc)
ISBN 978-1-4814-6180-1 (pbk)
ISBN 978-1-4814-6182-5 (eBook)

CONTENTS

Chapter 1: The Start of Something Sweet   5

Chapter 2: Cookies Catch On in America   16

Chapter 3: Celebrating with Cookies   24

Chapter 4: Our Cookie Culture   36

But Wait . . . There's More!   41

CHAPTER 1
The Start of Something Sweet

You've eaten lots of cookies, right?
You've probably chomped on a chocolate
chip cookie after lunch or munched on
a macaroon when you got home from
school. You might have even dunked a
lemon sandwich cookie in your milk before
bedtime. Yum! So you know a thing or two
about how good these sweet treats are.
But do you know how the cookie was first
created? Or why we call these little goodies
cookies? Do you know how the tradition of
leaving cookies for Santa got started? Or
what the world's favorite cookie is?

That's where this book comes in. By the time you finish reading this book, you will know the answers to all these questions and more. You will be a History of Fun Stuff Expert on cookies!

The history of cookies probably began ten thousand years ago with something that resembled crackers. The earliest known farmers mixed grain with water to make a paste. They baked the paste on sun-warmed rocks. It was a convenient and portable meal, if not exactly tasty.

EGGS
BUTTER
CREAM
FRUIT
HONEY

BAKE
IN CLAY
OVEN

Then, in the 600s in Persia, now called
Iran, bakers enhanced the grain-and-water
paste. They added things like eggs,
butter, cream, fruit, honey, and eventually
sugar. But they weren't making crackers
anymore, and they weren't making
cookies—yet.

They were making cakes. They baked
these cakes in clay ovens heated by
wood fires. It was hard to determine
the temperature in these ovens. So the
bakers dropped a bit of batter in them as
a test. These tiny test cakes became treats
themselves—what we would now call
cookies.

During the Middle Ages, (the period in European history between about the years 500 and 1500), cookie recipes and baking techniques spread. People traveled from Persia to western and northern Europe, bringing with them new spices to trade. Soon cinnamon, nutmeg, ginger, and anise were flavoring cookies.

By the 1400s, cookbooks included lots of cookie recipes. People in France could buy sweet wafers from street vendors in Paris. Cookies were becoming more convenient!

In the eighteenth and nineteenth centuries several things happened that made cookies even more popular. The prices of sugar and flour fell. And bakers could buy ingredients like baking soda and baking powder to make cookies rise, or puff up.

Before 1850 recipes used salt or baking ammonia to give cookies lift. Baking ammonia came from ground-up deer horns. After 1850 cookie bakers could simply buy baking powder and baking soda at their local markets.

BAKING SUPPLIES

During the same time period, ovens moved indoors and began to be made of metal, rather than clay bricks. In the early 1900s oven thermostats became the norm, allowing bakers to bake at precise temperatures. No more scorched sugar cookies! These innovations helped make cookie baking easier and faster. And the number of cookie recipes and home bakers took off!

By the early 1900s kitchen technology improved. Refrigerators could be found in many homes. Now bakers all over the world could store their sweets for more than a few days before they spoiled.

CHAPTER 2
Cookies Catch On in America

Dutch and English immigrants introduced cookies to the American colonies in the 1600s. In America we know cookies as thin, sweet, handheld desserts. They can be crunchy or chewy, plain or with toppings. They can include dried fruit, peanut butter, or even potato chips! The variations are endless. But no matter what ingredients they contain, we call them all cookies.

That's not so in other parts of the world! The English call cookies biscuits. No one knows for sure why we refer to them differently. But some people believe that after the American Revolution we wanted to separate ourselves from everything British. One way to do that was to use the word "cookie" from the Dutch *koeptje* or *koekje [COOK-yeh]*, which means "small cake," instead of "biscuit" from the British.

From the 1600s through the 1800s cookies were baked as special treats, not as everyday desserts. Back then you couldn't just open the cookie jar and sneak a couple of snickerdoodles. Ingredients and sweeteners were expensive. And cookies took time and effort to make.

Some early popular cookies are still made today. Spiced butter cookies called jumbles were a big hit, as were macaroons made from egg whites and sweetened coconut. Beginning as early as the 1700s, cookbooks contained recipes for these treats. Gingerbread cookies were also popular. They were cheaper to make than other cookies because they used molasses rather than sugar. In America molasses was much less expensive than sugar.

But even though kitchen technology was improving and ingredients were easier to get in the nineteenth century, the cookie supply was still limited in America. Families had to spend time baking cookies at home or buy imported cookies from England.

Then, around 1865, Belcher and
Larrabee, a New York company that
originally produced crackers, brought over
machines and methods to make cookies
in factories. Local markets began stocking
their shelves with these delectable treats.

In the late 1890s the National Biscuit Company, now Nabisco, made it even easier for the popularity of cookies to spread. They introduced wrapping and packaging machines. These machines were designed to help cracker products stay fresh while they traveled from factories to stores.

Then cookie companies latched onto them, and presto! The packaged, long-lasting cookie was born. Now cookies could be baked in factories in New York, shipped across the US, and sold in grocery stores out west. Yee-haw!

CHAPTER 3
Celebrating with Cookies

For centuries people have celebrated special occasions with cookies. What's a graduation party or a church picnic without a plate of oatmeal raisin cookies? But celebrating with cookies may be most closely associated with Christmas. So how did the tradition of baking cookies at Christmas begin?

Long before Christmas was even celebrated, people in many countries held festivals to mark the changing of the seasons. Ancient Romans held winter festivals as far back as 217 BCE! Fruits and nuts were served.

By the Middle Ages people in Europe celebrated Christmas, and cookies had replaced fruit as the treat of choice. Remember the spices like nutmeg, cinnamon, and ginger that came to Europe from Persia? They also became part of the cookies that people would pile on heaping trays for friends and family.

A few centuries later Queen Elizabeth I of England got in on the fun. In the late 1500s she had gingerbread cookies made in the shapes of her favorite advisers. Sweet!

Colonial Americans continued the tradition of cookie gift giving. When immigrants came to America in the 1600s, they brought recipes, baking techniques, and fancy cookie molds. By the twentieth century, molds were easy to buy. Americans were shaping cookie dough into stars and Christmas bells for family, friends, and Santa Claus!

And speaking of the jolly old fellow, how did the tradition of leaving cookies for Santa actually begin?

It all began in fourth-century Greece. Christians there celebrated Saint Nicholas on a special day each year, December 6. As Christianity spread to other countries, so did Saint Nicholas Day.

In the Netherlands, Saint Nicholas is called *Sinterklaas* [SIN-ter-class]. The night before his celebration, he rides through town on a horse. Children put out carrots for his horse, and he leaves presents in return.

In the 1600s immigrants brought this tradition from the Netherlands to North America. Children began leaving carrots for Santa Claus's reindeer on Christmas Eve. As cookies became more popular, they were added as a treat for Santa himself.

This fun tradition became especially important during the 1930s, when the Great Depression hit America. It was a time of record-high unemployment, bank closures, and low wages. Americans were down on their luck. Baking cookies for Santa was an inexpensive way for families to hold on to the hope of better times ahead.

For Santa

One of the most popular cookies to come along during the Great Depression was the chocolate chip. Though some people think it was created by accident—that bits of chocolate toppled into cookie dough—the chocolate chip cookie was probably well planned. It was created around 1938 by Ruth Wakefield of Whitman, Massachusetts.

The Toll House Chocolate Crunch Cookie, named for the restaurant Ruth owned with her husband, became a huge hit. The Toll House Inn had been serving butterscotch cookies with ice cream for dessert. But Ms. Wakefield thought a change would be good. She broke up Nestlé's semisweet chocolate bars and added them to her butterscotch cookie recipe.

The popularity of Ms. Wakefield's cookies increased when America entered World War II. Women were encouraged to send cookies overseas to "that soldier boy of yours," as one Nestlé ad put it. Until the war chocolate chip cookies had largely been an East Coast trend. After the war they were as popular across the US as apple pie. Eventually, Ms. Wakefield's recipe was printed on every Nestlé's semisweet bar and chocolate morsels package. Ms. Wakefield was one smart cookie!

1933 – FIRST OFFICIAL SALE

GIRL SCOUT COOKIES

1936 – BEGIN USING COMMERCIAL BAKERIES

GIRL SCOUT COOKIES

And speaking of smart cookies, the Girl Scouts of the USA know a thing or two about these sweet treats. Every year they sell nearly $800 million dollars' worth of Thin Mints, Samoas, and the other varieties. That's a lot of dough! The Girl Scouts used to sell cookies they baked themselves, but they began using professional bakers in 1936. Organizations like baseball teams and marching bands help fund their programs with cookies.

1939 - CREATION OF THE THIN MINT

G.S. COOKIES THIN MINTS

2015 - FIRST GLUTEN-FREE COOKIES

GIRL SCOUT COOKIES

CHAPTER 4
Our Cookie Culture

Today cookies come in all shapes, sizes, and flavors. Drop cookies, like oatmeal and chocolate chip, are dropped onto baking sheets. Bar cookies, like brownies, are baked in a pan and cut into squares. The dough for rolled-out cookies is stiff and perfect for cutting into Christmas shapes. Refrigerator cookie dough can be kept cold until you're ready to bake the cookies.

Molded cookies, like madeleines (MAH-de-lens), are baked in special molds. And sandwich cookies, like Oreos, use a cream frosting or filling to hold two cookies together.

As for flavors, there are countless cookie recipes! As railroads chugged west in the early 1800s, ingredients that reflected geography were added to cookies. Coconut flakes came from the South. Oranges were added from the West. Invented by the Kellogg brothers around 1900, cornflakes from Michigan made their way into cookie recipes. *Crunch!*

With so many cookie flavors, you may wonder what the world's favorite cookie is. The answer? The Nabisco Oreo! A stack of all the Oreos ever made would reach to the moon and back five times! The National Biscuit Company sold its first Oreo to a New Jersey grocer in March 1912. Over the years the size of Oreos has grown and shrunk, and the cream filling has changed. But the cookie's popularity has never wavered. Of course, Oreos aren't the only cookies in the cookie jar!

Take the animal cracker, which isn't really a cracker. The cookies' colorful red boxes were originally designed by Nabisco as Christmas tree ornaments. But the cookies sold well beyond the holiday season.

Fig Newtons were popularized by Kennedy Biscuit Works. The company named the cookie after a nearby town, Newton, Massachusetts. And

the Japanese probably created the fortune cookie that Americans eat with their Chinese meals. Let's hope the future of cookies has even more tasty twists!

HISTORY OF FUN STUFF

EXPERT ON COOKIES

Congratulations! You've come to the end of this book. You're now an official History of Fun Stuff Expert on cookies. Go ahead and impress your friends and family with all the delicious things you know about these treats. And the next time you need to satisfy your sweet tooth, grab a cold glass of milk and a cookie, and enjoy!

Hey, kids! Now that you're an expert on the history of cookies, turn the page to learn even more about these delightful goodies, plus some geography, science, and math along the way!

A World of Cookies

Americans eat a *lot* of different types of cookies, although you could say that Oreos and chocolate chip cookies are two of the most common. Let's take a little trip and look at some of the other most common cookies from around the world!

Latin America: Alfajores [ahl-fah-HOH-rehs]
Traditional alfajores, which were introduced to Latin America by the Spanish, are made of two cookies sandwiched together with **dulce de leche** [DOOL-say day LAY-chay]. Dulce de leche is very similar to caramel, both in color and in sweetness, and it's very popular in many Latin American desserts. Alfajores can be eaten plain, but they can also be rolled in coconut, sprinkled with powdered sugar, or even dipped in chocolate. Yum!

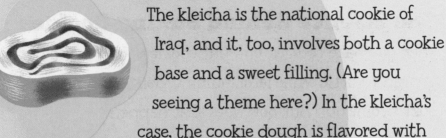

Iraq: Kleicha [CLAY-cha]

The kleicha is the national cookie of Iraq, and it, too, involves both a cookie base and a sweet filling. (Are you seeing a theme here?) In the kleicha's case, the cookie dough is flavored with different spices, and the most popular fillings include nuts and sugar, dates, or coconut and sesame seeds.

Thailand: Khanom Kleeb Lamduan [CAN-om Cleeb Lam-due-ON]

These Thai cookies are made up of very simple ingredients, but they are shaped like little flowers. Traditionally, after they are baked, they are placed in a sealed container with a fragrant candle that gives them a unique scent.

France: Macarons [mack-a-RON]

You may have seen these pretty little French cookies in bakeries or specialty stores, as they've become popular in the US recently. Like alfajores and kleicha, macarons are sandwich cookies. The cookie part of macarons is made from ground almonds, egg whites, and sugar, and the filling can be made from buttercream, ganache (a mixture of chocolate and cream), or jam.

Let's Get Chemical:
The Science Behind Baking Cookies

When you bake cookies, you put cookie dough into a hot oven, and a little while later, yummy, delicious-smelling cookies come out! But how does that happen?

When cookie dough goes into the oven, a series of **chemical reactions** take place. A chemical reaction is what happens when one substance turns into another substance.

First the butter in the cookie dough melts. Butter is an **emulsion**, or a combination of two substances that don't naturally stay together. In butter these substances are water and fat, and they're held together by other dairy solids. But when butter melts, the water and fat separate, and the cookie starts to spread out. The water evaporates, changing from a liquid to a gas and expanding against the walls of the cookie.

As the temperature of the oven increases, the **proteins**, or large molecules that help the cells in our body function, in the eggs start to solidify—the same

44

way they do when you hard boil an egg. It becomes firm instead of runny. This gives structure to the dough, making it hard instead of soft.

Some of the water that remains inside the cookie dissolves the baking soda you added in, which is also known as **sodium bicarbonate**. Sodium bicarbonate then reacts with acids in the cookie dough to create a gas that leaves air-filled pockets in the cookie. This is what makes the cookie light and crispy!

One of the next things that occurs while the cookie is in the oven, above 285 degrees Fahrenheit, is the **Maillard reaction**. The proteins and sugars that are present in the cookie dough combine to give the cookies their light brown color.

And then the last chemical reaction that leads to a finished cookie is **caramelization**, in which sugar turns brown—and gives off that nutty, sweet aroma that lets you know your cookie is done!

When the cookies come out of the oven, it's time to chow down—but not until you let them cool, of course.

The Baking Equation

To bake cookies you need to follow a recipe, right? Well, sometimes recipes involve math. Take this ingredient list for chocolate chip cookies, for example. This is a pretty standard recipe; it makes three dozen, or thirty-six cookies. Perfect for bringing to share with the class! But what if you had to share with another class, too, and you needed seventy-two cookies? You could double the recipe! That means that you take the amount needed for each ingredient and multiply it by two. Then, when you mix together all the ingredients, you end up with double the amount of cookies. Let's try it:

2¼ cups all-purpose flour

½ teaspoon baking soda

1 cup (2 sticks) unsalted butter, room temperature

1 teaspoon salt

½ cup granulated sugar

1 cup packed light-brown sugar

2 teaspoons vanilla extract

2 large eggs

2 cups chocolate chips

On a separate sheet of paper, write down how much you would need of each ingredient if you were to double the recipe.

Answers: 4½ cups all-purpose flour, 1 teaspoon baking soda, 2 cups (4 sticks) unsalted butter, 2 teaspoons salt, 1 cup granulated sugar, 2 cups packed light-brown sugar, 4 teaspoons vanilla extract, 4 large eggs, 4 cups chocolate chips

And if you want to actually make these cookies, here's how to do it. Make sure to ask an adult for help!

1. Preheat your oven to 350 degrees Fahrenheit.

2. In a small bowl stir together the flour, baking soda, and salt. Set aside.

3. In a large bowl use an electric mixer to beat butter with granulated and brown sugar until light and fluffy, about two minutes.

4. Add the salt, vanilla, and eggs one at a time, beating after each egg.

5. Add the flour mixture to the large bowl a little bit at a time and mix until combined.

6. Stir in the chocolate chips.

7. Use a tablespoon to scoop out little balls of dough and place them about two inches apart on a baking sheet lined with parchment paper.

8. Bake for about eight to ten minutes, until cookies are golden around the edges.

9. Remove from the oven and let them cool on the baking sheet for two minutes.

10. Transfer the cookies to a wire cooling rack and let them cool completely before eating.

Being an expert on something means you can get an awesome score on a quiz on that subject! Take this

HISTORY OF COOKIES QUIZ

to see how much you've learned.

1. The earliest known farmers mixed _____ with water to make a paste that they baked on rocks warmed by the sun.

   a. butter   b. milk   c. water

2. In the 600s in _____ bakers made cakes in clay ovens.

   a. Persia   b. Japan   c. France

3. What two early-twentieth-century inventions made it easier to bake cookies at home?

   a. electric mixers   b. railroads and   c. oven thermostats and
      and doorbells   cookie cutters   refrigerators

4. From what language did Americans get our word for "cookie"?

   a. Spanish   b. Dutch   c. German

5. What do British people call cookies?

   a. biscuits   b. galletas   c. crackers

6. Why were gingerbread cookies cheaper to make than other kinds of cookies?

   a. People ate more of them.   b. They were tiny.   c. They didn't need sugar.

7. What are some gifts children used to leave out on Christmas Eve before they began leaving cookies?

   a. socks   b. coal   c. carrots

8. Who created the chocolate chip cookie?

   a. Santa Claus   b. Ruth Wakefield   c. Cindy Nestlé

9. In what year was the first Nabisco Oreo sold?

   a. 1925   b. 1912   c. 1972

Answers: 1. c   2. a   3. c   4. b   5. a   6. c   7. c   8. b   9. b

48